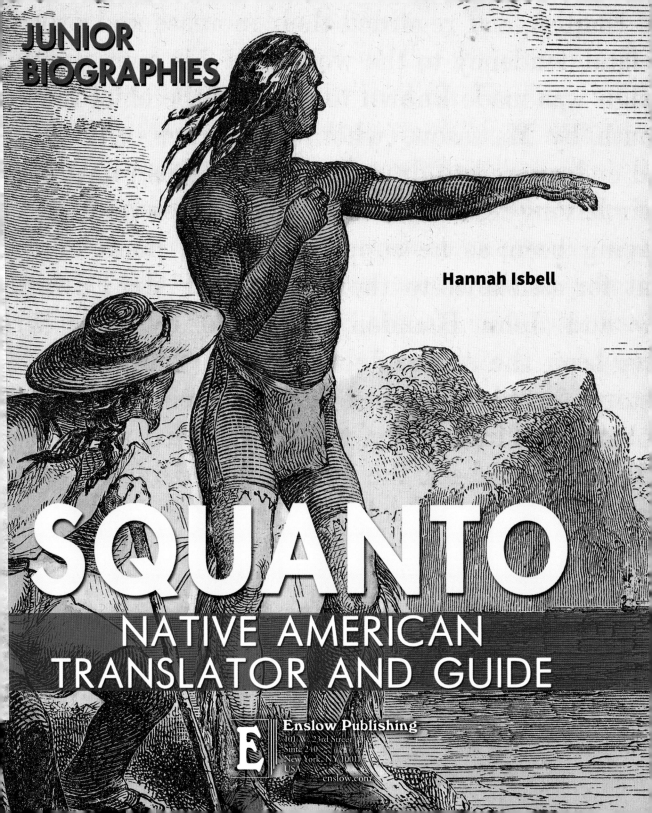

JUNIOR BIOGRAPHIES

Hannah Isbell

SQUANTO
NATIVE AMERICAN TRANSLATOR AND GUIDE

Enslow Publishing
101 W. 23rd Street
Suite 240
New York, NY 10011
USA
enslow.com

WORDS TO KNOW

agriculture Preparing and working the land for crops.

band A tribe; a group of native people with a shared culture.

expedition A trip that is made to explore or discover.

famine Deadly hunger in a large group of people.

Grand Sachem The leader of the Wampanoag people.

historian A person who studies history.

interpreter Someone who speaks more than one language and helps people communicate.

native Original.

plague A disease that kills many people.

plantation A large area with homes and many fields for planting.

savage A fierce creature; a word used by Europeans to describe native people whose ways they did not understand.

treaty An agreement.

CONTENTS

Squanto was a guide and interpreter for the English colonists.

CHAPTER 1
A MAN OF MYSTERY

The name Squanto is famous in American history. However, for a man who was so important to the country's history, much of his life is a mystery. What we do know is that Squanto, whose birth name was Tisquantum, lived a life of adventure.

During his life, Squanto was a slave, a prisoner, an explorer, an interpreter, and a teacher. He was the last of his people. But even as his own nation died out, he helped his people to start a new one.

THE PATUXET

Squanto was born around 1580, but no one is sure of the exact date. He was a Patuxet Indian. The Patuxet people were a band of the Wampanoag Nation, which was once where the states of Massachusetts and Maine are today.

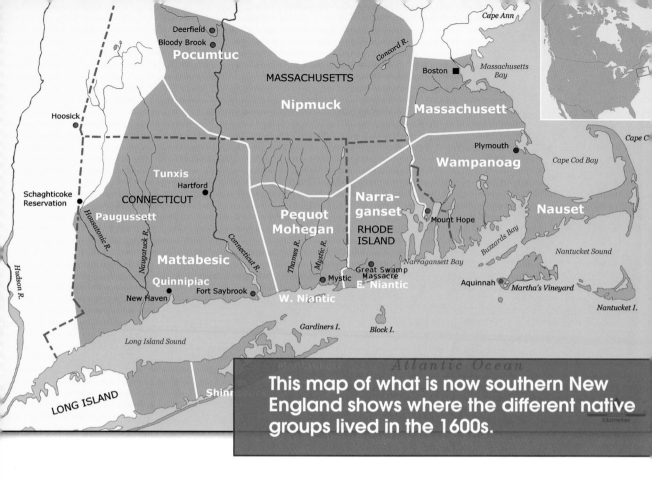

This map of what is now southern New England shows where the different native groups lived in the 1600s.

Not much is known about the Patuxet people, for sadly, they all died long ago. When Europeans came to North America, they brought diseases that killed most of the **native** people.

What we do know is that long ago, Patuxet was a place with busy cities and **plantations**. Their society was built around **agriculture**. The Patuxet hunted, fished, and traded with other nations, too.

In the sixteenth century, the native people of the Northeast had the most advanced agricultural methods in the world.

KIDNAP AND ESCAPE

Squanto was kidnapped many times in his life. Some **historians** believe that the first time Squanto was kidnapped, he was just a young boy. The story goes that he was brought to England, where he lived for many months before being returned home to Patuxet. However,

Captain John Smith was a famous English explorer. One of his men took Squanto and sold him as a slave.

no one knows for sure if this story is true. We do know that in 1614, an Englishman named Thomas Hunt, who worked for Captain John Smith, kidnapped Squanto.

Hunt promised to trade with Squanto. He talked him and twenty-six other people into going onto his ship. Once they were on board, Hunt locked them up and took them to Spain. There they were sold into slavery. Somehow, Squanto escaped and made

"Hunt, a worthless fellow of our nation ... more savage than they, seized upon the innocent creatures, that in confidence of his honesty put themselves in his hands."

Sir Ferdinando Gorges describes Squanto's kidnapping

his way to England. He was still a young man, but he had already been kidnapped at least once, been made a slave, and escaped. He also taught himself to speak English along the way!

Chapter 2
The Way Back Home

No one knows exactly how Squanto escaped slavery. Some believe Spanish holy men helped to free him. Others believe he did it on his own. Historians do know that he traveled to England, where a man named John Slaney gave him a job.

Slaney was very interested in exploring what Europeans called "the New World"—the Americas. In 1617 he sent Squanto on an **expedition** to Newfoundland, Canada. There he met another European explorer named Captain Thomas Dermer.

Captain Dermer traveled with Squanto back to his Patuxet home. Sadly, the home that he remembered was gone. While Squanto had been gone, a **plague** had killed all the people of his nation.

Smallpox was a terrible disease brought to the Americas by Europeans. The disease killed over 90 percent of Native American people between Columbus's voyage and the Pilgrim's landing at Plymouth.

In his early years, Squanto escaped slavery and traveled to England. He learned the language that later helped him guide the Pilgrims.

TRAVELS WITH DERMER

Squanto continued to travel with Thomas Dermer all over what is now New England. He worked as an interpreter and helped Dermer to explore the different nations. Together, they met many native North American people.

Not all the people were friendly to Squanto and Dermer. More people were learning about the illnesses brought by Europeans. Some thought that the explorers could not be trusted. In 1620, Dermer was captured by the Pakonet and Nameset people. He was only released after Squanto stepped in.

"[We] passed along the coast where [we] found some ancient plantations, not long since populous now utterly void. When [we] arrived at my savage's native country [we found] all dead."

Captain Thomas Dermer describes his trip with Squanto

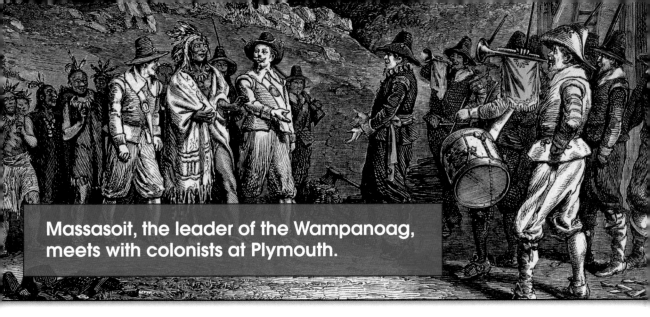

Massasoit, the leader of the Wampanoag, meets with colonists at Plymouth.

CAPTURED!

Squanto's friendship with Dermer made some people uneasy. The same year that he rescued Dermer from capture, the two were attacked. Dermer died from his wounds. Squanto was taken prisoner, this time by his own people, the Wampanoag.

A few months after his capture by the Wampanoag, the **Grand Sachem**, whose name was Massasoit, decided to test Squanto's English language skills.

CHAPTER 3
SQUANTO AND THE PILGRIMS

Grand Sachem Massasoit and the Wampanoag had been watching a group of English settlers who were living on the Patuxet's old land. One member of their nation, named Samoset, spoke a little English. He tried to make contact with the English people. Samoset learned that the people had suffered a terrible famine the previous winter. They were struggling to survive.

Today, we know this group of settlers as the Pilgrims. The Pilgrims called Squanto's native land Plymouth. Grand Sachem Massasoit sent Squanto to learn more about these new strangers.

MEETING THE PILGRIMS

When Squanto met the Pilgrims in March of 1621, they were having a hard time. When they settled in Squanto's

Samoset tried to speak with the Pilgrims when they arrived in Plymouth.

> "He was a special instrument sent by God for their good beyond their expectations."
>
> *William Bradford, a Plymouth colonist, praises Squanto*

old village in 1620, they were already weak and sick from their long journey from England. The Pilgrims suffered terribly during their first winter in North America. They did not know how to work the strange land, how to grow food, or the best ways to hunt and fish.

The Pilgrims land at Plymouth in 1620.

TEACHER AND TRANSLATOR

Squanto worked hard to help the Pilgrims. He was kind and patient with them. He earned their trust by teaching them the skills they needed to survive in their new home. One of his most important lessons to the Pilgrims was how to grow the Three Sisters: corn, squash, and beans. Squanto's people were experts at farming these crops, and with his help, the Pilgrims were finally able to grow food for themselves!

Early North American people had a special way of growing corn, beans, and squash. They planted all three together. The corn was a structure for the beans to climb, the beans made the soil richer, and the squash grew along the ground, keeping out weeds.

Chapter 4
Thanksgiving

Squanto also guided the Wampanoag people and the Pilgrims toward peace. With Squanto's help as interpreter, the two groups created a **treaty**. Massasoit honored the agreement until his death in 1661. In the treaty, the Wampanoag agreed to allow the Pilgrims to live on their land. In return, the Pilgrims agreed not to harm the Wampanoag people.

Harvest Celebration

In the fall of 1621, the settlers and the Wampanoag people celebrated their harvest with a feast. Ninety of Grand Sachem Massasoit's people, including Squanto,

Thanksgiving has been celebrated on and off since the first Thanksgiving. It was officially made a holiday by President Abraham Lincoln in 1863.

The Pilgrims celebrate the first Thanksgiving with the Wampanoag people in 1621.

brought five deer to the feast, and together with the Pilgrims, they partied for three days! We now recognize this as the first Thanksgiving, and it has become a symbol of peace and cooperation.

This bust of Squanto is on display at the Pilgrim Hall Museum in Plymouth, Massachusetts.

A Broken Peace

Sadly, the peace that the Wampanoag and Plymouth colonists made was not shared by others. As more Europeans arrived, the native people suffered. Still, Squanto worked the rest of his life trying to help the different groups work and live together.

"We are so far from want that we often wish you partakers of our plenty." (In other words, they had so much food that they wished more people would join them to celebrate!)

Edward Winslow writes about the first Thanksgiving

TIMELINE

1585 Squanto, first named Tisquantum, was probably born around this time.

1614 The first certain record of Squanto, when he was kidnapped by Thomas Hunt.

1614–1617 A plague kills all of Squanto's tribe while he is away.

1617 Squanto escapes slavery and starts working for an English explorer, Thomas Dermer.

1620 Dermer is killed and the Wampanoag people capture Squanto.

1621 The Plymouth colonists and Wampanoag people celebrate what would come to be known as the first Thanksgiving.

1622 Squanto becomes ill and dies, and the Patuxet people die out.

BOOKS

Gilman, Sarah. *The First Thanksgiving*. New York, NY: Enslow Publishing, 2016.

Hooks, Gwendolyn. *If You Were a Kid at the First Thanksgiving*. New York, NY: Children's Press, 2017.

Stanley, Joseph. *Wampanoag*. New York, NY: PowerKids Press, 2016.

WEBSITES

The First Thanksgiving
kids.nationalgeographic.com/explore/history/first-thanksgiving/
Get the facts about what did (and did not!) happen at the First Thanksgiving.

Squanto Biography
www.biography.com/people/squanto-9491327
Learn all about the amazing life of Squanto.

INDEX

Published in 2018 by Enslow Publishing, LLC.
101 W. 23rd Street, Suite 240, New York, NY 10011

Library of Congress Cataloging-in-Publication Data
Names: Isbell, Hannah, author.
Title: Squanto: Native American translator and guide / Hannah Isbell.
Description: New York : Enslow Publishing, 2018. | Series: Junior biographies | Includes bibliographical references and index. | Audience: Grades 3–5.
Identifiers: LCCN 2017021464| ISBN 9780766090668 (library bound) | ISBN 9780766090651 (pbk.) | ISBN 9780766090682 (6 pack)
Subjects: LCSH: Squanto—Juvenile literature. | Wampanoag Indians—Biography—Juvenile literature. | Pilgrims (New Plymouth Colony)—Juvenile literature.
Classification: LCC E99.W2 I73 2018 | DDC 974.4/00497 [B]—dc23
LC record available at https://lccn.loc.gov/2017021464

Printed in China

To Our Readers: We have done our best to make sure all website addresses in this book were active and appropriate when we went to press. However, the author and the publisher have no control over and assume no liability for the material available on those websites or on any websites they may link to. Any comments or suggestions can be sent by e-mail to customerservice@enslow.com.

Photo Credits: Cover, pp. 1, 4 Kean Collection/Archive Photos/Getty Images; pp. 2, 3, 22, 23, 24, back cover (curves graphic) Alena Kazlouskaya/Shutterstock.com; p. 6 Nikater, adapted to English by Hydrargyrum/Wikimedia Commons/File:Tribal_Territories_ Southern_New_England.png/CC BY-SA 3.0; p. 8 Stock Montage/Archive Photos/Getty Images; p. 11 Peter Newark Pictures/ Bridgeman Images; p. 13 Stefano Bianchetti/Corbis Historical/Getty Images; p. 15 Archive Photos/Getty Images; p. 16 Lambert/ Hulton Fine Art Collection/Getty Images; p. 19 Barney Burstein/Corbis Historical/Getty Images; p. 20 © AP Images; interior page bottoms (folk pattern) Irtsya/Shutterstock.com.